Little Sea Horse and the Big Crab

D1494789

by **Anne Giulieri**
illustrated by **Omar Aranda**

Look at Little Sea Horse.
She is going in and out
of the coral.

"I am hungry,"
said Little Sea Horse,
and off she went
to look for food.

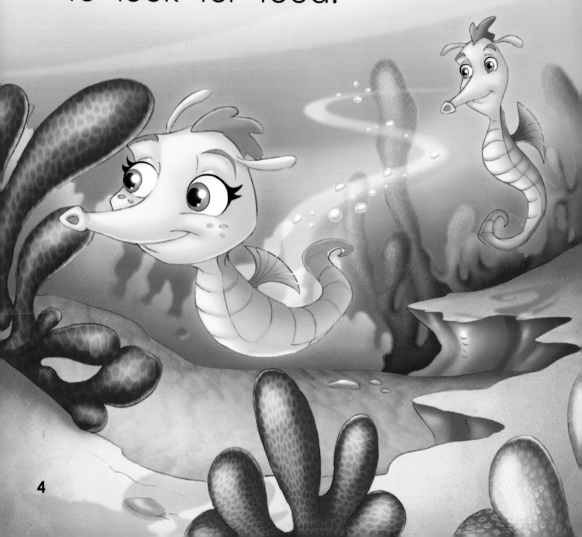

"Where is Little Sea Horse?"
cried Father Sea Horse.
"Oh, no!
She is outside the cave."

Little Sea Horse looked
inside the cave.
"I will get food in here!"
said Little Sea Horse.

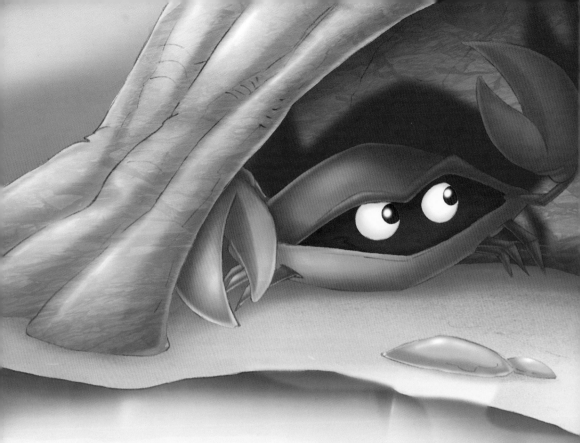

"**Stop!**" cried Father Sea Horse. "You can not go inside the cave.
Big Crab is in the cave. She will **eat** you!"

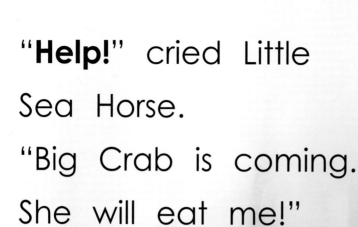

"**Help!**" cried Little
Sea Horse.
"Big Crab is coming.
She will eat me!"

Father Sea Horse
went after Little Sea Horse.
"Get out of the cave!"
he said.

"Little Sea Horse,"
said Father Sea Horse.
"You have to swim
with me."

"I will swim with you,"
said Little Sea Horse.
"Big Crab will **not** eat me!"

Little Sea Horse
went with her father,
and she did not go in
the cave again.